DANA PLATO'S RETREAT

David Schwartz and Jessica True
Dana Plato's Retreat

Published by Spines
ISBN: 979-8-89569-863-1

Dana Plato's Retreat

3rd Edition

David Schwartz

Jessica True

Contents

Dedication

This book is dedicated to the man who lost his life at David's bikini car wash.

A Message from David Schwartz

To all my fans, although I've been called the most interesting man in the world, I've always believed that if you can dream it, you can do it. Men who want to be me will love this book. Men who are jealous of me will hate it. Women who don't believe in a double standard, who love life, and love adventure, love me. Women who are prudes or old-fashioned hate me. I cater to people who love life and want to experience everything life has to offer. Love me or love to hate me. This is America, and I will fight for your right to freedom of thought and speech.

CHAPTER DESCRIPTIONS

CHAPTER ONE: The three move in together, Dana, David, and Jessie, into the swinger's club living quarters. David and Dana get engaged to be married.

CHAPTER TWO: Dana Plato Porno Director. Dana and David fight about racism, which contributes to their break up. David is arrested and pleads his case in court.

CHAPTER THREE: Time travels back to when they met. Dana's **'inner course.'** Dana recruiting vid

CHAPTER FOUR: David's empire and conquests.

CHAPTER FIVE: David and Jessie reunite and reminisce.

1. Do It Like Dana

This book is a true story. Some names have been changed to protect the guilty.

Fort Grant, Arizona prison

Movie producer, entrepreneur David Schwartz, sits in a prison truck with the Arizona chain gang outside the window.

DAVID

Running a swinger's club in Phoenix was just like the TV show *Cheers*. We had our Cliff and our Norm and all the other regulars, except our regulars were all undercover cops. They would sit around, watch porn, watch people have sex, dildos flying, almost getting hit with a vibrator. But what the hell did I get myself into? I mean, how did it all begin? I remember watching on TV Dana getting arrested for robbing a video store. She ended up double paroled because she also wrote a fake prescription for Valium. That's when Dana came to me for help. I really felt sorry for her.

Why did I pick Phoenix as the location for the swinger's club? Well, because it's close to L.A. I knew I could get movie people out here easily. I had been growing my business too fast and was too well known in Vegas by now. The Vegas cops were jealous of me and had been harassing me. So I had to get out of Vegas because of their low mentality. When I first came to Phoenix, I opened a bikini car wash - two actually; one on Van Buren and the other in Scottsdale. In 40 days we had 40 car accidents.

Due to the car accidents that my bikini car wash caused, the Phoenix cops passed an ordinance banning sexy outfits outside of a business. The ban included holding signs that advertised a bikini car wash because the sexy signs likewise caused sexual arousal car accidents. What I had done was advertise the bikini car wash on the G-string of the models and they would bend over toward traffic. Well, somebody ended up getting killed. The man had stopped to look and another gawker crashed into him going 40 mph. He died right in the driveway of the bikini car wash. He was slumped over in his seat with blood coming out of his mouth. I figured now would be a good time to close it down, now that we started killing people. We almost decided to make it into a movie called *The Bikini Car Wash Massacre*, but people died before we could start it. So yeah, that business closed down pretty quickly.

I had to do something, so I decided to try opening a swinger's club.

Picture of David Schwartz: The show Dallas was popular at this time. David wore $2000 alligator skin boots and a $100,000 belt buckle to look like J.R. Ewing. This Stetson hat is initialed in gold.

1994: 1040 E. Indian School Road, Phoenix, Arizona

It was at this time that Dana called me and asked what's up. I pitched her the idea for the two of us to open a kind of Playboy mansion. My plan was to cater to celebrities and investors. Our place never catered to sleaze bags like the Phoenix cops claimed it did. Even the cops ended up coming and enjoying our place, but unfortunately, they were only coming to arrest me.

One night, there were a bunch of guys sitting around in the orgy room and no women showed up. When they complained, I told them, *"Well, you shouldn't have come on gay night. Ha-ha!"* One guy wanted a refund, and I took him outside so he could get his money back. But once we were outside, he assumed a karate position as if he was going to karate chop me.

He went into the crane position from *The Karate Kid*. I said, *"What are you doing?"* He said, *"I want a refund."* Shit, he spoke like some Kung Fu master. I mimicked him and took a karate position too. I shouted, *"Boy Scouts! But you're still getting your refund."* I don't really know karate. I told him I was still going to give him his money back whether we fought or not.

I don't believe I ever became a drug addict, but I did heavy lines at this time because I had to be awake 18 hours a day to run the club. Guys paid $35 at the door. Women and couples got in for free. I always gave customers their money back if they weren't satisfied. Dana and my girl, Jessie, read from a pitch that I wrote for answering the phones. Both

Jessie and Dana sat at the front desk as customers came and went. I instructed them to tell the caller that they would introduce him to their friends. It made it look like there were a lot of women there. There weren't.

DANA (answering in a professional but friendly tone)

Are you calling about the fantasy photo shoots or the adult parties at night? Yeah, we have models available for nude pictures that will pose any way you want them to. Then we have a swinger's party for open-minded males, females, and couples.

Tonight, we have TV star Dana Plato coming over to sign autographs. So, we have to limit the number of single men and the only way to get in is to put your name on the VIP list.

DAVID

Dana had to cover the front desk whenever Jessie was asleep. One morning, Dana got impatient for Jessie to wake up and take over the phone. She wanted to give Jessie a line to wake her up so she'd start working. I was out of drugs at the moment. So Dana decided to crush up a line of aspirin and give it to Jessie, hoping it would look like real drugs. Well, she woke Jessie up and gave her the line of aspirin. Jessie snorted the powder. I was about to go run and hide and say, *"I didn't do it! It was her!"* But Jessie never noticed. Dana was like, *"Fuck that girl! I'm not giving anyone real crystal when I'm on probation."*

JESSIE

Dana had been giving me crushed up lines of Aspirin instead of real drugs; she confessed later. The three of us - Dana, David and me - lived together in one house at 1040 E. Indian School Road in Phoenix. Dana and I slept in the same bed for three months on the master bedroom mattress because it was a small office/house with living quarters. It was a swanky dive in a low-class neighborhood, very grunge, very edgy.

DAVID

I would nap and have sex in the master bedroom while Jessie covered the front desk. The sleeping arrangement never prevented me from having sex with Dana every day. After Jessie moved out, I started sleeping in the bed with Dana every night and having threesomes with Dana and a chick named Lisa. I also put a king size bed in another room I named the orgy room. This bed could fit about 6 people. Women started coming from faraway places just to have sex with me and Dana.

JESSIE

At the first meeting, Dana cooed over me as if I was an adorable, new puppy. She did everything to make me feel included, equal and loved. I did feel like we bonded. That sweetness that you see in her *Diff'rent Strokes* character is her real personality.

David had crashed my car and it was totaled. This left the three of us, me, Dana, and David, without transportation most of the time. David would hoof it to fast food joints to bring food home for Dana and me.

When I walked with David to get fast food, we were approached by beggars. David would ask the beggar for a dollar before the beggar could ask. This, he said, was a good strategy for avoiding beggars and if you wanted to have fun, if a person asked for money, just say, *"I'll give you money, but you have to promise that it will only go for liquor."*

DAVID

If you ever want to make a beggar happy, tell him the money can only go for booze or drugs.

JESSIE

Dana would always dance with the black guys. She wanted to be the Different Strokes daughter forever. I loved it when any black man came into the club, Dana would jump up and dance with him, dorky white girl style.

A fallen TV star hosting a swinger's club is a big deal for the state of Arizona. This is a confessional story. There were mistakes, regrets, heartaches, as well as successes.

At the end of one of her singing solos, Dana felt herself up provocatively. She slid the palm of her hand up on top of her breast and then cupping it, her hand slowly glided. That was so seductive, more so than her voice. The camera did a super close up of her mouth so that all you saw was Dana blowing a kiss. Then she stuck out her tongue. The video camera did a close up of her sexy tongue wag.

Dana flashed the camera one bare tata and showed off her perfectly ripped midriff and tan. She was never afraid, never embarrassed, the opposite of me.

1994: Dana flashing her bare tata.

JESSIE

David created a stage name for me in the club, Jessie James. David didn't like me using my real name in the club. Years later, a porn star took the name Jessie James. I'm not her. But I played this Jessie James character for David and Dana's club venue. My stage name was a gimmick to get more customers into the nightclub. I was only the receptionist, actually. And I was the boss' girl, his property, no cheating allowed on my part. Nothing sexual ever happened between Dana and me. She was a perfect gentleman.

1994: Nicknamed Jessie James in the club (Jessica True)

JESSIE

There was the time David tried to do a 24/7, 5-day swinger's party. It was pretty grandiose. David collapsed into the bed somewhere during the event. He went unconscious for almost a full day. I feared he might be dead. We couldn't wake him up though we tried. I was almost crying with worry when David got up and said his favorite joke after sex, *"Quick, give me your face."* I was so happy he wasn't dead!

DAVID

I don't even remember that.

JESSIE

There was this one time that Dana tried to kiss me. We were both sitting on the bed having a heart to heart. She moved her face in really close to mine, but I jerked my head away. I avoided her kiss just in time. It was awkward. I stood up and backed away from her before she could plant one on me. I'm not gay. She understood and said that she was there for me if I ever changed my mind. I was relieved that she wasn't angry at me for turning her down. But then she said she thought she had better examine me to make sure I wasn't born a boy. She seemed like she only had a medical concern for looking between my legs, like it was all a friendly taking of the temperature or something. I wanted to prove to her that I wasn't born a boy. I didn't see the harm in letting her examine me buck naked. I didn't suspect her and didn't think she might have an ulterior motive. Now looking back, I realize I fell for her trick. She only did that exam so she could see me naked. I can't believe I fell for that! She had a way of tricking me into things I wouldn't consent to otherwise. I can say now that she was very good at manipulating me.

DAVID

Dana was kind of a sexual predator. But I wanted Jessie to refrain from other men in order to make her seem unattainable, to project a superstar image for her.

JESSIE

Dana was around 29 and I was only 22. I thought living in a swingers' club with Dana Plato was the best gig ever! All I knew was that I was being put with Dana to headline a club and it was the biggest thing that ever happened to me. That's what I thought at that age.

A swinger's club is exactly like a dance club except there is pornography on the TV screen and patrons drank beer out of a cooler. David blasted classic rock on the large speakers, and there was a lot of dancing. The interior was extremely dark. The beautiful Arizona spring was good for outdoor sitting. Patrons stood around outside the door as well. David's swinger's club was kind of like where Austin Powers would go, but not quite as shagadellic. These kinds of clubs were common in the '90s. Many sports figures visited our club. I didn't recognize anyone because I don't follow sports.

David never used Dana or me for his nude modeling business. We only headlined his night club.

A politician and his wife were always in attendance. I won't say who. He would hang out and chat with me at the front desk where Dana signed autographs. Meanwhile, his beautiful blond wife with hair down to her butt would take men outside and sit with them in cars.

Dana Plato

These three pictures of Dana were taken by David's personal photographer.

DAVID

There was a time that Dana needed money to pay for her plastic surgery. Six different nips and tucks and enhancements and so forth that she got done. Dana wanted her boobs done, and I had a doctor who would do it in exchange for using her name. But Dana also wanted to have her eyes, nose, and butt done and that was too much for the guy to agree to do for free. So she called her trust fund and told them that she was in a car accident to get money out of the trust. Dana actually told her trust fund that the car accident had made her severely disfigured. I said, *"You look almost as good as right before you had it done."* She went from an A cup to a B cup, which was stupid.

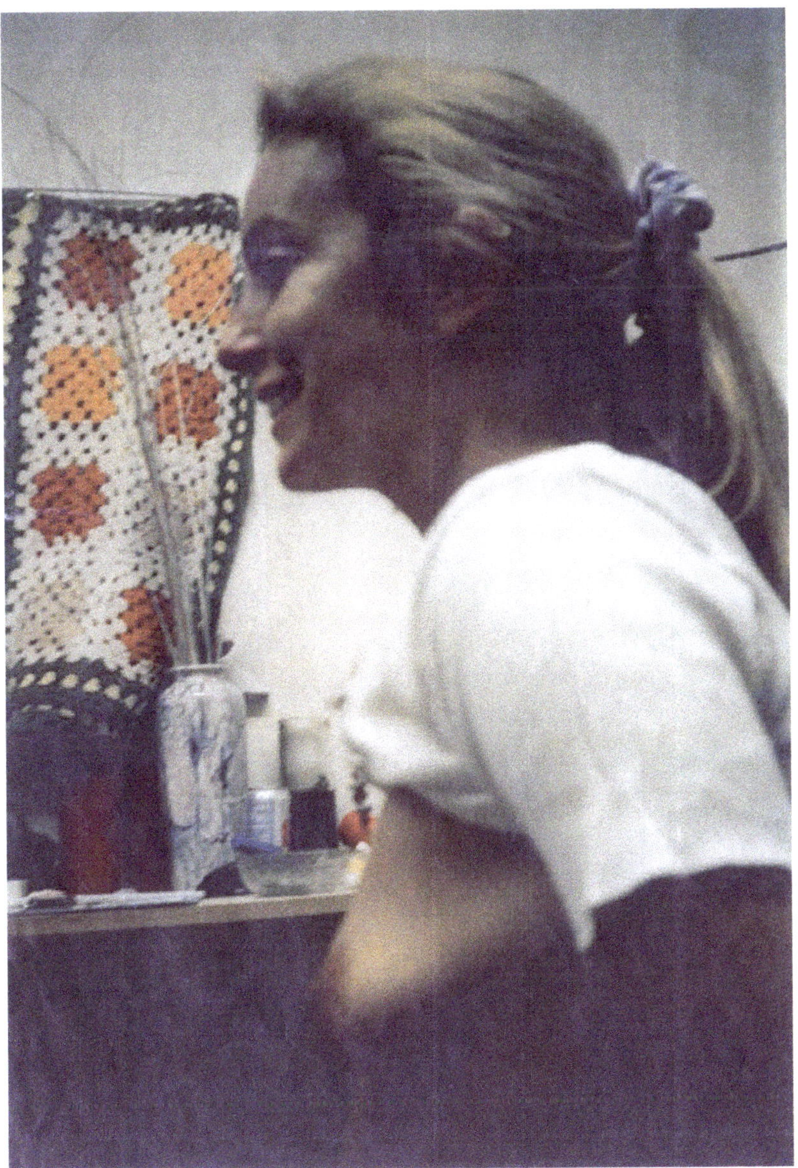

1994: David took a picture of Dana's breasts before surgery just
in case they screwed it up.

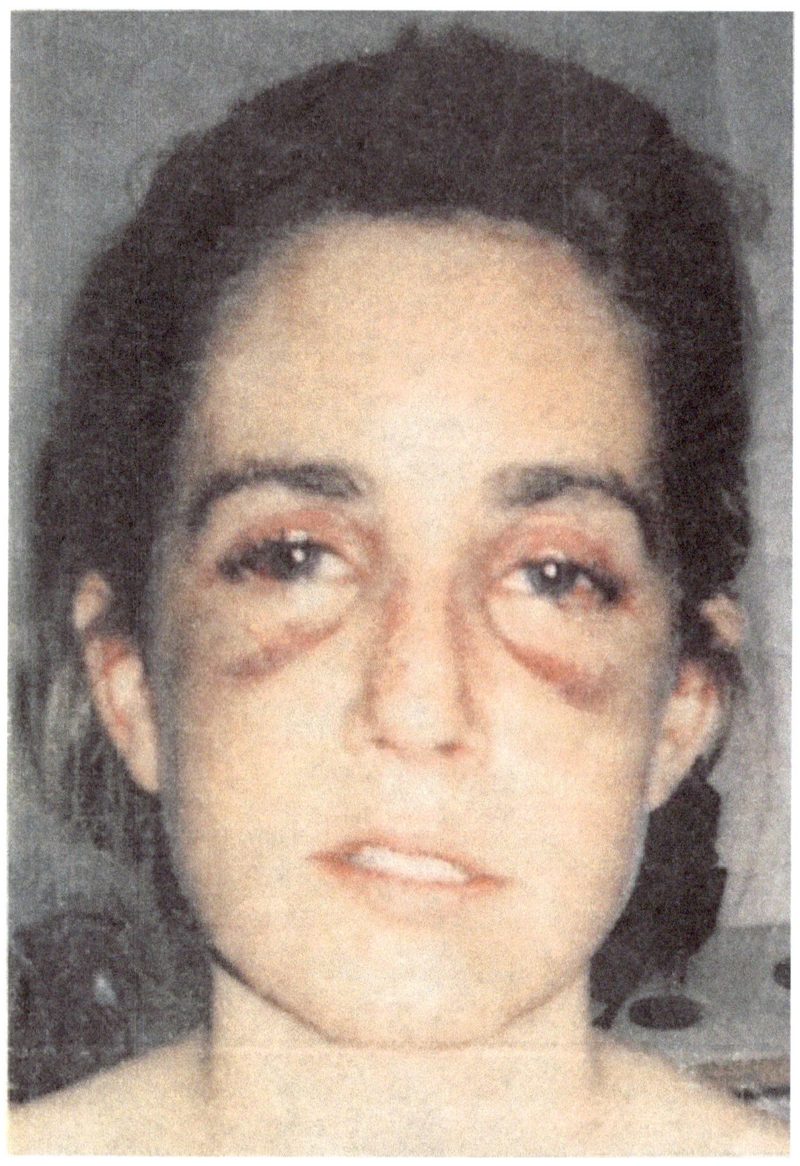

1994: David took this picture of Dana's face one hour after cosmetic surgery.

JESSIE

Another one of David's sales gimmicks was to use this picture of Dana after her surgery on the back cover of this book to create intrigue. It looks like she was beaten up and on drugs or something. But Dana was actually the only one of the three of us that wasn't on drugs in 1994. She took her parole seriously. She never even drank alcohol. The black eyes are post-operative, not punches.

I took care of Dana during her recovery from plastic surgery. She was a 10 on a 10 scale and didn't really need it. Dana started sleeping with the club attorney because she and David had an open relationship. She said she hoped he would pay for her surgery, but that didn't work out for her. This lawyer guy was so coked up that his jaw got too stiff for him to even talk. I was embarrassed for him.

DAVID

Cops claimed the swinger's club was a house of prostitution, but the evidence shows that there was an undercover cop pretending to be a hooker who could never get fixed up.

The club attorney represented me after my arrest that year. But he showed up two hours late for court one time, even confessing to the judge that he overslept from partying the night before. Then he showed up to another court date without my defense papers, explaining that he set the defense papers on his car and they blew away. He also made a porno with a woman at the swinger's club, which the court was going to use to charge him with a count of prostitution if he didn't resign my case. A certain public defender who really wanted to watch that guy's porno decided to take my case. This public defender made zero effort to defend me.

JESSIE

David well knew that I didn't even like pornography. I have never been a swinger and never will be. I didn't know what the word even meant. Everyone knew that about me. So for him to put me on a flyer as host of a 24/7 swinger's party for 5 straight days is laughable. I was only living there because there was a celebrity living there. I love celebrities. I was young and dumb. So don't come up to me after this book comes out and tell me about your threesome because I was never into that. I realize today that it was a mistake for me to be living in a sex club as a platonic roommate, but I was a lost soul at that age. Also, to promote the club, David directed a pretend bondage picture of me. He assured me that it would be sexy. He told me to pretend to have my hands tied behind my back. It ended up scaring the shit out of my friends because they didn't know that I was only pretending to be tied up and it was semi-nude. David and I also made a sex tape of us on a shaggy animal skin rug.

1994: Picture of the Dynamic Duo: Dana Plato on right and
Jessica True on left.

1994: The swinger's club venue flyer advertisement

DAVID

I had a guy paint the club, but he painted it hot pink which I didn't like so much. The interior was amazing in black light, though. I had professional artists paint murals of Jessie and Dana on the walls inside the orgy room with ray guns in their hands. You should have seen the fluorescents. They looked like green Martians! The murals of Jessie and Dana were eight feet tall. There were bright stars and planets on the ceiling. It looked like a super cool planetarium. When people made love in there, it was like looking out over the universe. When you walked in, you felt like you were in another world. I hung plastic room dividers on wires. There's two ways of doing things, the million-dollar way and the creative way. The main artist was John Mapalo. He puts a picture into a projector and then paints it on the wall. Dana chose the picture of herself for the mural and she absolutely loved it!

JESSIE

I'm not trying to promote promiscuity. I'm just a journalist publishing a historic event for the state of Arizona is all. When David found 7 more VHS tapes in storage, I knew I had to add stills to the third edition. Got pictures of the interior walls of the swinger's club. You won't want to miss this sleazy mural art! It's awesome! Flying, naked creatures and volcanoes!

Mural of Dana on swinger's club wall

Mural of Jessie at swinger's club

DAVID

I enjoyed the cat and mouse chase with Jessie, but Jessie was happy whenever I was with Dana. When I was with Dana, Jessie would get a vacation from sex.

One time when Dana was covering the front desk, I prank called. I said to Dana, *"Gee, I've heard of Jessie James but who's Dana Plato?"* Jessie was an unknown local community theatre actress. I did that just to make Dana's heart sink.

JESSIE

I will never forget the night a nice lady with a cowboy hat sat with me at the front desk. She was really enjoying herself. But then her jealous, mean, violent husband came looking for her. She panicked and asked us to hide her. She hid in the bathroom, and we told her husband that she wasn't there. This husband pretended to leave and then he came charging in like a raging bull. He was the scariest man I have ever seen. He pounded the bathroom door and almost broke it. We were all scared to death! David was so brave. He grabbed the guy and said, *"Get out."* David personally escorted the man out of the door like he was nothing. David never even flinched. The rest of us were shaking in our boots.

Ever since that night, I have always thought that David was the strongest, bravest man I have ever met. Watching David throw that man out was like watching Steven Seagal. It's amazing that David did all his own bouncing. He never used a bouncer. He was it. Talk about brass nuts! If they make a movie about us, David should be played by Jon Voight or Christopher Walken or Nicholas Cage. David had a shaggy haircut with a porn star beard so I think these stars would look great playing him. David once told me that if you ever can't avoid fighting someone, at least try to pretend you are completely insane, like, scream as if you are a wild animal. Screaming produces adrenaline and scares the shit out of your opponent. Nobody wants to fight a person who seems crazy.

DAVID

I stopped fights by giving away free passes a lot. The place brought in about $7,000 a week. For a club that had just opened up, that was pretty good business. I noticed that a nerdy customer, Scott, was stealing from me. I tested him by putting something out where I could observe him taking it. So after the thing disappeared and he was the only one around, I knew he was the thief. I confronted him when nobody else was around. I said to him, *"Scott, something is missing. I know you took it."* I told him he had two choices: *"You could admit it or get off with me only beating the shit out of you till you bleed once. Or you can lie to me, and I'll beat the shit out of you till you bleed every time I see you."* I told him I would beat him for every lie he told. He denied stealing so I hit him and gave him a bloody face. He lied again so I knocked off his glasses. I said, *"This time I'm breaking your glasses in half."* And he said, *"Don't. They are expensive and new."* So I asked the question again, just to give him another chance, but he lied again, so I broke his glasses in half. Then he told the truth. Scott would lie and then after I smacked him bloody, he would tell the truth. He bled every time I smacked him. Every time I asked a new question, he would lie again. This happened about five times. You would think he would just tell the truth; he was getting the shit beaten out of him anyway.

After the fifth time, I backhanded him; he flew and landed next to a crowbar. I saw his shaky hand moving closer and closer to the crowbar. I said, *"Scott, you grab that crowbar, it will be your last move for the rest of your life."* So he grabbed the crowbar and dropped it. That's when he ran away and called the cops. I told the cops that I had caught him stealing, and he tried to beat me up. *"What'd he steal?"* they asked. I said, *"Stereo equipment and other knickknacks."* The cops asked him if he was stealing my stuff and he said yes, like some stupid idiot. They turned to him and said, *"You're under arrest."* So the cops ended up arresting Scott instead of me. I thought that was pretty funny. This reminds me of the old expression, "After death comes the doctor."

JESSIE

Dana's favorite songs were *Black Water* by the Doobie Brothers and *Because the Night* by Natalie Merchant. She sang them all the time. Dana changed the lyrics of *Because the Night*, so it would better suit her personality. The song goes, *"Come on now and try to understand the way I feel under your command."* Dana sang instead, *"...the way I feel I'm beyond command."* Dana was never under anyone's command. She was beyond command.

VHS tapes of Dana and me singing were shot in 1994 at the swinger's club, transferred to digital in 2018. I have put 7 videos of us on YouTube under the screenname *Dana's former roommate*. One video shows Dana cursing her mistakes and dropping the F-bomb. This is what happens to stars when they can't get enough work in show biz or a top agent. So many of her *Diff'rent Strokes* co-stars were already working normal jobs - no longer the stars of a TV show. Gary Coleman was working as a security guard, for example. It just makes me think we really need to treat our celebs better and stop tearing them down. Without celebs, there would be nothing to watch on TV or movies.

1994: Pic of Dana on right, Jessie on left

1994: Picture of David and Dana at the swinger's club

DAVID

Dana was fired from *Diff'rent Strokes* because she got pregnant. She had a crush on Todd Bridges during the taping of the show. Her loud announcement of her pregnancy was intended to make Todd jealous. She went around bragging about her pregnancy to everybody working on the set. She didn't count on losing her career. The producers just instantly took her into an office and fired her.

They said she can't play the role pregnant. They couldn't have a child on the most wholesome show in the world pregnant. After that, Dana spent a few years just raising her kid and working at some Las Vegas cleaners. One day she just walked next door to the video store. She held up the video store with a toy gun, but she was still a felon now. She wanted the publicity; it was like a cry for help.

JESSIE

Dana always looked like she was having an orgasm when she sang. She would ooo and mmm so great. She would make circles with her French manicured hand as she sang on the stage of the swinger's club. She requested a French manicure and valium when she arrived. David promptly arranged for us to take a trip to the mall to get it for her. The manicurist said it was an honor to have Dana there and thanked her. She ended up liking my song better and decided to sing it too. Then we sang it together as a duet; the song was On and On by Stephen Bishop. Dana directed the whole thing. David dressed me in a white bejeweled jacket, Neil Diamond style, for the duet with Dana.

My singing was worse than Yoko Ono and Dana was intentionally lisping like Natalie Merchant. No wonder Dana killed herself. When I heard the playback, I wanted to kill myself. David should have taped us doing skits instead of singing. Both of us were actresses after all, not singers. We were like *Dumb and Dumber*, silly girls at a slumber party. But we had great chemistry and excited smiles for each other as we sang together. Our eyes lit up with childish glee. She'd blow me a kiss.

So we could put on a good show together. Dana would always hold up a finger and ask for one more chance to sing the song better. To this day, whenever I have to get back up from some failure, I give it my Dana finger, "One more time!" It's actually fun to hear a star hitting wrong notes. David did phenomenal work on production. He dressed me in a cowbell top, my best color really. I have always looked great in cow. At Cowtown, David took pictures of me in his sparkly purple dress pointing rifles menacingly, sexy kick butt style; it was dazzling. These guns and dresses were wardrobe items that David owned. David hired a production crew that had worked for Michael Jackson and told Dana and me that we were very close to getting a record deal.

Dana Plato was a great role model. Just kidding! This lifestyle really doesn't work. You either get into recovery or you die. And David's lifestyle was like Jurassic Park where the T-rex always gets out and you never have control. This lifestyle is like the dinner scene in Temple of Doom.

There was a phone conversation between Dana and her son, Tyler, that I remember. Tyler was in Oklahoma back then. Her son begged his mother to come home. He was crying on the call. When she hung up, Dana told me that she hated the way her son would make her feel guilty. She had lived with her ex-husband there in Oklahoma for a little while.

I asked her what it was like to work with Gary Coleman. She told me he was a little crazy.

She lifted her shirt casually and flashed her tatas, all the time telling me her stories. It was a thing with her. She would play it off like she was just adjusting her blouse or something. I realize now that it was intentional. David also wore a purple, shiny silk shirt with some chest hairs showing. He also had some bling that impressed people.

Dana walked around the club with a full house of people wearing an unbuttoned blouse and a black bra underneath. I don't mean it was half buttoned up or something - no, it was unbuttoned all the way. The shirt only covered her shoulders.

At this time when everyone was so high on drugs, David's 1989 horror movie, Las Vegas Blood Bath, was taken by some paranoid tweakers to be a real snuff film and rumors spread. This made David even more proud of his work than ever before. He assured me that the cast was all still alive. But sometimes David said in a spooky voice, *"They still haven't found some of the cast members...in one piece, that is."*

DAVID

It is listed as *"Biggest horror movie shot in Vegas."* I also directed and produced the movie *American Revenge* in 1988.

JESSIE

One of the patrons at the club took a pepperoni stick out of his cowboy hat and offered me a slice. I must have been drunk, so I ate it. David blasted me for that. David warned me that I could get pubic hair lice from eating it. David was right. Eating salami slices out of a guy's hat is very unhygienic. I'm lucky I didn't die of some infection.

DAVID

The guy probably really wanted Jessie to lick his Italian salami.

JESSIE

There was only one bathroom for the entire place. A community towel hung by the sink - again, to be used by all in attendance. David nicknamed this towel 'the cum towel.' One time David took a shower and forgot his towel. He didn't want to have to dry off using the 'cum towel' so he begged me to let him use my towel just that once. But I refused to let David use my towel. I was concerned about hygiene and didn't like sharing towels with anyone. So that one time David was forced to dry off using the cum towel. He was so pissed at me.

DAVID (yelling at Jessie)

You make me dry off with the *"cum towel,"* and yet you ate a salami out of a guy's hat!

JESSIE

The club was actually an old flower shop that David had rented. There was an office area where people came in and went out. There was a large living room area with a couch. There was a party or orgy room. Then there was a bedroom where Dana and I slept. So it was kind of a house, kind of an office. We lived and we worked there as well. The neighborhood was kind of seedy.

Like I said before, Dana and David had no form of transportation. My friend, Chris Rabalais, was called to drive Dana home from the tattoo parlor. He said it was such an honor to meet her that he pretended not to be grossed out by her new tattoo.

DAVID

One night someone took a crap on my floor. Then I fired one security guy who then told me I couldn't fire him. I asked why not? He answered because he is just going to be here every night anyway so I might as well let him keep his job. My security guy, Tony, fell asleep on the job sometimes. To teach him a lesson, one time I took everything out of the place and woke him up. I screamed at the top of my lungs, *"Tony, what happened?"* He woke up, rubbing his eyes and looking confused as hell. When he saw that the place was empty, he totally freaked out. He took off running and never came back. Well, he shouldn't have fallen asleep with lines of crystal and beer cans everywhere. That's what happened when my security guy tweaked on crystal meth for days on end.

When I first opened the club in the Spring of '94, I couldn't get any business. Every time a car would pull in the parking lot, they would be scared off by the fact that they were the only car in a dark parking lot. Nobody wanted to be the first one to go in alone. The empty parking lot frightened people. I started telling people to park at the Indian bar next door, the Ponderosa. The Ponderosa was always packed full of Indians.

That's how I was finally able to get a crowd in my parking lot. Also, the Indians started wondering over after the last call. They could keep drinking at my place.

There was a nude model who wore a tampon to a fantasy photo shoot. The string was hanging between her legs. It looked like a mouse tail, like she had a mouse up there. She jumped around the blue wall with the string dangling all over the place.

We also had a regular girl from Romania who called herself a nice girl. But I had to kick her out for prostituting herself. She was always asking me if she could wear my costumes. I told her no. I didn't want her to get guacamole or sour cream on them. Guacamole and sour cream go great on real tacos, but not on hers. By the way, if God didn't want us to eat pussy, he wouldn't have made it look like a taco.

Also, one time a Native American man came into the club at 3 am. He said his brother had hung himself in the place where my club was. There had been sightings of ghosts around by many people. The tenant who moved in after me actually died in this building as well. We should actually call this place the Amityville Whore House because there were two deaths, many apparitions sighted, and everyone felt compelled to do things they wouldn't normally do here. There seemed to be ghostly power in the building making us all do things for the first time that we never even dreamed of.

JESSIE

My time at David's club came to a tragic end. David had been keeping me up all night working at the front desk. He wouldn't let me sleep and would wake me up early in the morning to work the front desk. He just wouldn't let me sleep. He kept waking me. Finally, after about three months, I couldn't get out of bed. Dana called my mom to come to get me. I was in a trance-like state as Dana walked me to mom's car and laid me in the back seat with a pillow. I barely recall this. Dana almost carried me out to the car that day. I slept at Mom's house a couple of days. Then Dana called and told me to come back to work. I didn't return her phone call because I wasn't fully rested yet. If I were sane, I would have just gotten my own apartment. That way I could get a good night sleep and work a shift that was comfortable and not so bad for my health. David paid well. But moving out and living in my apartment would have made too much sense. I wasn't thinking clearly. As soon as I was rested, I very much wanted to return Dana's call and go back to work for her. Sanity had returned, I guess. But by this time the club had been shut down by cops and Dana was gone. I had blown my opportunity to stay with Dana. I will always remember how she told me she wanted to take me away from David and be my manager.

She said all David could do was put me in B movies, and she could do better for me than him. She told me to give her time to get her career back. Dana was a wonderful, kind, caring, loving human being.

When Mom picked me up at the swinger's club, she saw a four-foot-tall framed picture of me hanging over the couch in the living room. In the picture, I was semi-nude and pretending to have my hands tied behind my back. My mother was so frightened by that picture that after David was arrested, she went down to the jail and requested the police forbid David to ever contact me again. And her request was granted. It became a condition of David's parole that he never contact me. When I was a teenager, I had turned down a role in a movie because the role required nudity. My mother wanted to be this big, liberal mom and send me to a Playboy Magazine audition (thankfully, I was rejected). I went through a phase in my life where I posed nude for anyone that wanted me to without any discrimination. I went from turning down nudity roles in movies to dropping my clothes for anyone that asked. I outgrew that phase, thank God!

Of course, none of this stuff in this book is something I would do today. If a celebrity manager came up to me today and asked me to pose semi-nude, pretending to have my hands tied in order to promote a swinger's club, I would say no. What I considered an honor at age 22 would definitely be something I would turn down today. I would say, *"Thanks but no thanks."*

JESSIE

I was pissed off at Dana for calling Jessie's mom to get her out of the club. I think Dana lied to Jessie to get all of my movie roles for herself and take advantage of my contacts.

George had introduced me to a director in Scandinavia where they were looking for a female lead to play opposite Kiefer Sutherland, among other things. I had put out a press release saying Jessie was getting that part.

JESSIE

I don't believe a star was worried about me getting her B roles, especially not singing roles. She was so kind to me after I sang like a dying cat. We had a real, true friendship.

It killed Dana that the media ignored her antics and she would be thrilled that we are publishing it all now. She didn't do these crazy things to be hidden in private. We would publish this story even if Dana was still alive because her death is irrelevant to our story. This is our fun, sexy story of living in a club with a star, not a bio of Dana. But when people find out all about Dana's shenanigans, they will love her even more.

DAVID

The place got raided twice. They said I could open the place back up as long as I didn't serve alcohol. I didn't have a liquor license. But two weeks later they were leveling the same misdemeanor charges at me plus they were now calling it felony prostitution. I assured them I wouldn't sell alcohol. I gave out sodas instead. So the guys had to sit around in a swinger's club drinking soda. I told Dana not to get any tattoos, but she went and got a bunch more tattoos. Dana was naïve and stupid like that. She was close to illiterate because she couldn't really spell or write.

Sometimes she had me sign her name instead of doing her own autographs. I planned to get Dana a part in a porn film now that she was happy about her new cosmetic surgery. We planned to tell the media that Dana was begging for her porn NOT to be released.

If Dana pretended that she didn't want people to see her porn, it would sell more. It's a fact that if someone says 'Hey, watch my porn,' nobody will want to watch it. But if someone says they DON'T want their porn to be seen, people will be lining up by the dozens. They'd buy it for big bucks. The porn that I made for Dana was eventually destroyed by the cops.

Dana and I used to leave the door cracked so people could see in just a peek. But they really didn't see anything that was going on.

One time while Dana was sleeping, I put a toy rat between her legs. Then I told her to be careful because there are mice in the room. She removed the covers and started screaming. There were two Rottweilers that a lady brought and they became part of the club. Two girls would have sex with the dogs, a preacher's daughter and a cop's daughter. This was a turn on to Dana and me because it was so taboo. We used to think, 'Look at Daddy's little girls being mega sluts.' Did you ever meet a girl who was so wholesome, it made you sick?

Everything with Dana was falling into place. Dana told me she loved me. I told her we could get engaged if she wanted. I proposed to her and she accepted. We got engaged. Before we married, we decided to move the club into a mansion.

Collage of Dana and Jessie 1994

2. The Amityville Whorehouse

DAVID

I tell all my best stories on the sperm of the moment. I told Dana that her kitty looked like a caterpillar and she better trim into a butterfly.

Another service that I offered was making pornos of couples. Dana wanted in on the action. One time she offered to be the director. That day I had two ladies scheduled who were best friends and they both brought their new boyfriends.

I announced to the clients that I had a big treat for them, that their porno was going to be shot by the famous TV star Dana Plato from *Diff'rent Strokes*. They were ecstatic and said it was an honor and a turn on. They all started drinking and doing lines of meth.

One couple started banging away in every position. The other guy got major erectile dysfunction. Dana made the situation worse by asking the guy when he was going to get his tiny thing up. His girlfriend said we should see how big his thing can get. And Dana said, *"Well, when's it gonna get hard?"* Dana's comments made it impossible for the guy to get hard. The couple turned red from embarrassment and they ended up breaking up their relationship. Then the two best friends ended up becoming enemies. I told Dana it was all her fault for making those comments. Dana's reply was, *"OH well. Another one bites the dust."*

Dana and I were planning to move the club into a mansion. We found a wealthy investor willing to put up $100,000 as a down payment for it.

I warned Dana that this guy was a racist redneck. I said to her, *"You shouldn't dance with any black guys in front of him."* I know what it looks like, but I'm not a racist. The thing is if you want to do business with someone – anyone – then you have to avoid offending him. Dana blew the whole deal by giving the guy an anti-racist speech. She went on and on about how prejudiced I was and how low I was. Turns out, he was the racist one, not me.

I arranged for some other movie producers to meet with Dana. But on the day they were coming to interview her for a big part, the redneck investor friend of ours yelled, *"Who wants to go tubing down the river?"*

Dana shouted back, *"I do! I do!"*

I told Dana not to go tubing that day. She knew we had the movie people coming at 2 pm. I knew the whole thing was irresponsible and careless and would just end up blowing our appointment. I also warned Dana not to go out with the guy until after he put up the money he promised us. If she went out with him before he put up the money, it would be like a prostitute putting out before getting paid. I explained this to Dana.

Well, Dana went tubing down the river in spite of me asking her not to. He didn't just take her tubing. He took her around to about ten different friends' houses with his arm around her, bragging about who she was saying stuff like: *"Look who I am with!"*

They didn't get back until 3:30 – well past the appointment time. Dana was all sunburned. The movie people came and went without meeting her or talking with her. In the end, she made *me* look unprofessional.

And to top it all off, our racist redneck investor friend decided that he didn't need to put up the money after all. He felt like he had made friends with Dana and that the prestige of her friendship was all he needed. He had already taken her around to all his friends so the thrill was gone. So the $100,000 we were supposed to get from him was blown. He didn't actually refuse to put up the money, but I told him I didn't want his money after he tried to turn things around and call me racist.

I told Dana I never wanted to work with her again. I threw her out of the house. I told her that we were through.

She called many times after that, crying and begging for another chance. She left a card for me to read. It said, *"David, I'm sorry, I love you."*

I called her on the phone and told her, *"Forget it, Dana. You're too stupid for me."*

After the break-up, Dana tried to keep the part in the movie with the producer, George. This was the same movie I had fired her from. She went to see George in person and pleaded with him to let her stay. George told her there was nothing he could do to help her figuring since I was the executive producer of that movie. George had to tell her that she was fired.

This was the last I heard from her. A few years later she killed herself by overdosing on Valium and Loritab.

Dana feeling herself up

Pic of Dana in jean shorts on stage of swinger's club.

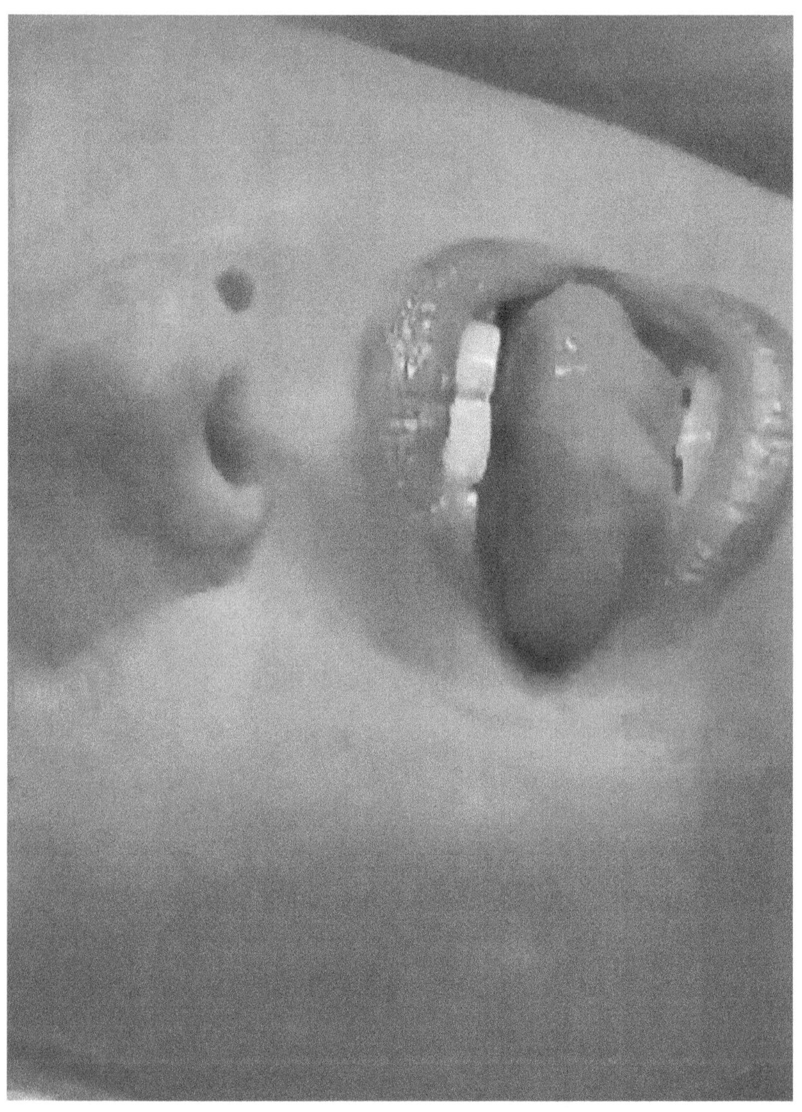

Dana's French kisses to the camera

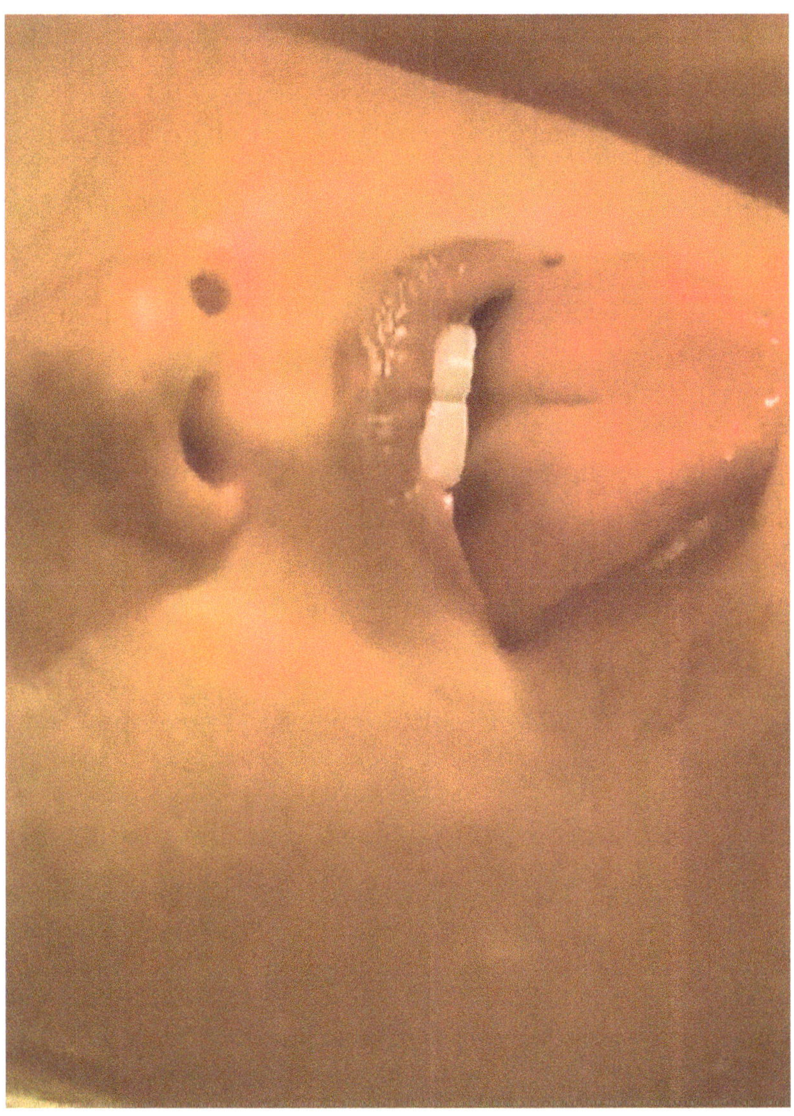

Meantime, I found a replacement for Jessie at the front desk, Debbie. And now that Dana was gone, Debbie became the new queen bee. I called Debbie *"Bobby Dylan"*. She had the habit of getting high on meth for days and then falling asleep somewhere. I got especially angry every time she would fall into a comatose sleep in the orgy room. A scantily clad woman asleep in the orgy room just isn't safe.

I told her a bunch of times, *"Don't fall asleep in the orgy room!"*

Despite my repeated warnings, she again fell asleep in the orgy room.

So I decided to teach her a lesson. There was no other way she was going to understand. Pedro, the security guy, was also passed out nearby. I put semen on her chest while she was unconscious and unzipped Pedro's pants and then woke her up. She saw the semen and said, *"Oh, no, I've been raped. Call the police."*

I said, *"Who did it, Debbie? Was it a five-foot penis? Look. Was it Pedro?"*

She looked at Pedro lying there with unzipped pants and freaked out. Pedro looked like the stereotype of the fat Mexican with the sombrero walking the donkey. He also had a big smile on his face from drinking.

I said, *"Let's reenact the scene of the crime for the police, Debbie. What did he do, Debbie? Did he get behind you? Did he pull your hair back?"* I pulled her hair back. *"Did he grab your boobs, Debbie, and squeeze your nipples like this, Debbie?"* I grabbed her boobs and squeezed her. *"Did he bend you over and start fucking you like this, Debbie?"* And then I kept going. She ended up having an orgasm by my reenactment of the crime.

The girls in the office told Debbie that it was me that was back there with her, so she figured it out that I was pranking her. She came to me pissed off and threw a punch at my face. She didn't hit me, but it was so close that I could feel the hairs on her fingers. When she missed me, she missed hitting one of the girls' kids' face. Her swing just missed the little kid who was watching. She missed the kid by an eyelash, and I ducked out of the way.

If you met a sailor and fell in love would you go out with him? Does that mean you like semen? Apparently, Debbie loves semen because it was all over her.

My friend, George, was an Emmy winning movie producer. He was also the head trainer for a famous football team who I can't name because I have to protect their privacy. George brought his entire team to the club and Debbie went home with them one time. She didn't want to talk about what happened, but I noticed her butt was sore and bloody. She could barely walk. She limped for a week. I think she had butt sex with every single one of them. Her ass saw more action than the NFL.

Debbie wasn't supposed to be cheating on me so when she disappeared for hours one time, I asked where she was for all that time. She claimed she was raped. I said if she was raped, there could be a possibility of pregnancy or disease. She answered, *"No, the rapist used a rubber."*

I said to her, *"Debbie, you're fighting like crazy and he's on top of you. Did he say, 'Wait, hold on a minute, I gotta put a rubber on?'"*

Then I asked, *"Did he hold you down with one hand while the other hand was putting on the rubber? It takes two hands to put a rubber on. How is that possible unless you were helping him?"*

Then she confessed that she'd had consensual sex with this guy. She said she was sorry. And she told me why she did it. She said, *"You were with all these pretty girls, and I was afraid you were going to dump me, so I wanted to protect my feelings by cheating on you."* Yeah, that's what she said – that's Debbie for you.

I told her I'd rather be with a nice-looking girl that allows me to be with all the beautiful women in the world rather than be with the most gorgeous girl in the world where sex could become boring.

The final end of the swinger's club came at the time we had Stephanie coming in – she was actually a female undercover cop only pretending to be a hooker. I tried to get rid of her like I always do whenever I find a prostitute on the premises. There were no prostitutes allowed in the club. I banned anyone caught prostituting in my club. I kindly tried to send her to Las Vegas, but she was sticking to the place like some kind of old gum.

Any model who wants to work for me doing stills for patrons has to show me her breasts to prove that she's not a cop. A cop will never show their breasts. Stephanie showed me only one breast because her other breast had a police wire. The police department had to manipulate the prostitution charge because there was no real basis for it.

Stephanie had given me her picture 3 different times after I kept putting her pictures in the closet to get rid of them. She kept bothering me to fix her up, but I never did. There are only two reasons she never got fixed up, A. She was so ugly that it was impossible. B. I wasn't running a house of prostitution.

During the argument with the female undercover cop, every undercover cop in the club decided to arrest me right then and there for fear they wouldn't get another opportunity.

The undercover cop pretending to be the prostitute – I like to call her 'the ugly, wicked witch of the Wizard of Oz with the big nose' – I said to her, *"The club doesn't allow hookers."* I had told her that so many times and I was tired of her pushing me into those conversations. As soon as I said that, she knew it would destroy her case. So she said to the other cops, *"Arrest him!"*

It was like a scene in the movie The Fugitive. Cars came from everywhere. Helicopters appeared overhead. All the undercover cops high fived each other as I was cuffed.

I had named my club *The Unknown*. So when they dragged me out in cuffs, one of the cops said to me, *"You're not unknown anymore."*

I said, *"Hey if it weren't for you guys each paying $35 per night, I would have had to close down five months ago. Your business kept the club open."*

They charged me with 11 felonies. I ended up doing three years in prison. They said my ads for models violated the state's escort laws and providing beer without a liquor license was another count against me.

If any woman made any money in my club, I never got a piece of it. But apparently, the cops got a woman to lie and say she was giving me a cut from her johns.

The undercover cop, Stephanie, had tracked down Tina who was a hooker that I had banned from the club for hooking. Tina was disgruntled so she lied to the cops and told them I was getting a cut from all the hookers there.

The cops left my club unlocked. The place was looted and vandalized.

Also, there's a law that says the cops can destroy a convicts' property if the convict doesn't respond to a notice to do so within 30 days. The cops sent the notice to the club knowing full well that I was in jail and couldn't respond to it.

The property that the cops destroyed was about 20 million dollars' worth of pictures and videos, including rare footage that I had of Michael Jackson. Jessie and Dana lost pics at this time as well. I filed a lawsuit against the Phoenix police department for destroying my property, but I lost. I found out that the cops had started investigating my club at the behest of my ex-wife who I was divorcing. She had found out that I was running a swinger's club and living with

Dana Plato and Jessie in Arizona. She wanted to get full custody of my kids, so she came up with a plan to put me in prison. So it was her that had called the cops and said, *"David Schwartz is known to be in the adult industry, and Dana Plato is on probation for holding up a video store, and they are running a house of prostitution."*

My ex-wife also said we were shooting pornography using underage girls even though there was no truth whatsoever to that statement. She was lying through her teeth. After a couple months of investigation, when the cops couldn't find anything wrong, they decided to come to the club disguised as undercover movie producers. The undercover cops hired one of the models at my agency to do a nude photo shoot. They instructed her to dance and striptease. They told her to masturbate with a dildo for their video that they were directing for their own use in the future. When the video turned up in court, the video zoomed in on the model's butthole which took up the whole screen. You could see what she had for lunch and dinner. It was the most tasteless video I've ever seen. Can you imagine a big screen shot of a butthole? It was in very poor taste, but remember the undercover police directed and shot the video.

After they shot the video, they found out that one girl masturbating did not violate the prostitution law. The law states that it takes two people to manipulate the genitals under a fee agreement to constitute prostitution.

They had to go back to my club and video two girls having sex with each other. The law, California vs. Freeman, states pornography is not prostitution. So then the cops hired two of my models to do the video. They were supposed to be adult movie producers, yet they used the terminology, *"Take this artificial penis and insert it into the other girl's vagina."* Medical terminology. No adult industry professional would use that kind of terminology. Normally guys would say 'take this dildo and fuck her with it' or something like that.

When they were done shooting the video, they went to their car and then they remembered they forgot to pay. Without paying there would be no crime. It was the first time those models ever did a video like that. They went back and paid the front desk. The models told them not to tell me that they did anything extra because they were afraid they would get fired.

I'm the only person in the country that ever did time for the crime that the police created. Nobody else ever went to prison for a porno movie that the police department shot. My case became a published case of law.

The difference between escort and modeling is the following; if a girl comes to your house naked, you need an escort license. But if you take pictures or video of the girl, then it falls under the category of modeling.

I had been to the state modeling board and asked if I needed a license. They said no. I had that same official show up in court, and she was asked the same question there. In court, she lied. She lied and said any time a girl gets naked, it doesn't make a difference if there was a camera or not.

This was at the time Madonna came out with her sex book pictures. This official said Madonna would need an escort license to do that in Phoenix, which is a lie.

So, like I said, when they showed the video in court, it was a full-screen shot of a woman's butthole. The prosecutor said how disgusting it was.

I had the undercover detective on the witness stand, Detective Sterling. I'll never forget that name. The prosecutor's name was Cahill. One of my charges was advertising for an escort without a license. That's when I asked Sterling what my ad had stated. He said the ad read; girls available for fantasy videos and stills. I asked him if that refers to the girl's fantasy or the photographer's fantasy.

He admitted it was the photographer's fantasy. Then I asked if he had acted upon himself when he shot the video, not authorized by the Phoenix police department. He answered that he was indeed acting on behalf of the Phoenix police department, not by himself. So I said, *"I agree that this is truly the most disgusting video I've ever seen. But it is correct to assume that the video you shot represents the fantasy of the Phoenix police department."*

The prosecutor objected. She accused me of harassing the witness. Before the judge could answer, I moved on to the next statement knowing that I got that in.

The model does what she is told to do. The patron chooses

the fantasy. I told the court, *"So will you all agree that this video represents the fantasy of the Phoenix Police Department?"*

3. Dana and David in Las Vegas

1991

Welcome to the Jenny Jones TV Show

JENNY

Today's show will cover jealous wives whose husbands are in the entertainment business. Today, we have David Schwartz as our guest. Mr. Schwartz is an entrepreneur, movie producer and also publisher of a modeling magazine. He owns many companies, all of which deal with beautiful women. His beautiful wife Rebecca does not trust him. On one of David's magazines, his wife Rebecca is on the cover. But guess what? His girlfriend Ann is on the back.

What do you have to say about that, David?

(David is about 40 years old. He has a muscular build. He is wearing an expensive Versace black suit with silver threading. He is also wearing a few hundred thousand dollars worth of jewelry)

David Schwartz

DAVID

Hi, Jenny. To answer your question, Ann only became my girlfriend *after* the magazine was published and after Rebecca and I had become separated.

JENNY

Your wife claims you are surrounded by beautiful women all day long, and she doesn't trust you. Tell me how you spend your average day, David.

DAVID

Well, Jenny, I have about 50 people working in my office.

When I walk into my office, I say hello to the secretary at the front desk. Then I go to my plush office, and my private secretary brings me my coffee.

JENNY

Woah, wait a minute...

DAVID

What do you mean wait a minute? What's wrong?

JENNY

Whatchya mean your private secretary brings your coffee?

DAVID

That's right, she does. What's wrong with that?

JENNY

Why don'tchya get your own coffee?

DAVID

Well, let me ask you this, Jenny, who gets you your coffee?

JENNY

(In a bragging tone)

I get my own coffee!

DAVID

Well, I'll tell you what Jenny, if you ever work with me, when you get your coffee you can bring me mine.

JENNY

Your wife Rebecca claims you are sleeping around. What do you have to say to that?

DAVID

Honest Jenny, I have never cheated on my wife. And if I'm lying let God strike me dead. (All of a sudden a light bulb pops, *"it was like the worst timing in the world!"*). God, I swear I'm telling the truth!

DAVID

Jenny contacted Elizabeth Taylor and told her that her picture was in one of my so-called *"sleazy"* magazines. She suggested Elizabeth Taylor sue me. And Liz did sue me, but she lost.

Flashback to the time when David met Dana

DAVID

When my girlfriend, Ann, expressed an interest in bailing Dana out of jail so that we could party with her, I asked Ann if she was a carpet muncher or a tile cutter. Ann asked, *"What's the difference?"*

I answered, *"A tile cutter is a carpet muncher minus the fur."*

We wanted to bail Dana out of Clark County Detention Center, but Wayne Newton beat us to it.

I was making $50,000 a week, just living life. I had a hundred gorgeous girls working for me. I had my own limousine.

After Dana got paroled again, she got her own show at the Rio called Tropical Heat. This show took place right after her court date. Dana pleaded guilty and got double probation. Luckily, she had a top attorney who later became the district attorney for Las Vegas.

This show called *Tropical Heat* turned out to be a big bomb. It lasted only two weeks.

Also, a condition of her probation was that she stay employed. I thought to myself this is meant to be. When we first met, Dana told me, *"If anyone can help me back to Hollywood it would be you."*

I said, *"Yes and I'll take good care of you."*

I thought it was fate that I had been trying to bail her out and she ended up coming to me. A top entertainment director brought her to me right when her show got canceled at the Rio in Vegas.

There's like a one in a million chance or coincidence for something like that to happen!

I had Dana follow me to my office. My office is filled with action pictures from my movies and magazine stories on me. Even I was impressed every time I walked into my office.

I told Dana, *"I can't believe that you could ever rob a video store."*

Dana told me how her manager had stolen over $700,000 from her. When she had robbed the video store, she had held it up with an obviously fake gun. It was basically a cry for help.

DANA

Please, David. I need a job, or I will violate my probation. Everyone has abandoned me, and no one believes in me. Besides the job, I also need a real friend.

DAVID

I said, "Dana, I loved watching *Diff'rent Strokes*."

Actually, I never saw it, but I knew of Gary Coleman. I was also contacted by Todd Bridge's (*Diff'rent Strokes* character Willis) friend, Ron Long, to do a music video of Todd. Ron Long was the son of famous song writer Shorty Long who wrote *Here Comes the Judge* among other famous songs. Todd Bridges had a great voice and he had recorded himself singing a song called *Ladies of the Night*. The song sounded phenomenal. I played the song for the patrons at my swinger's club in 1994. Jessie also loved it. But before Todd and I could put a contract together, Todd went to prison.

I knew word was traveling fast that Dana Plato was in my office. I told Dana I had two jobs available. One was a worker job like everyone else that paid $300 per week. The other one was the job of a manager/personal assistant (or you could abbreviate personal assistant and just put pussy assistant) that paid $1000 per week.

She said, *"What does a worker job entail?"*

I told her, *"Dumping the garbage, cleaning up the office and getting everyone coffee."*

She said, *"What does the manager's job entail?"*

I said, *"Are you open-minded?"*

DANA

I sure am.

DAVID

It starts at $1000 per week, and you would be second in charge. You would do interviews and PR. You would also take care of all my sexual fantasies, and I would take care of all your sexual and financial needs.

I said, *"Which one are you interested in?"*

DANA

I'd like the personal assistant job.

DAVID

I told Dana, *"There are two courses. You have a choice to take one of them."*

DANA

I'm ready. What are they?

DAVID

The first one is the outer course. That takes about a month before you get paid. The second one is the inner course. That will get you started faster with an advance salary.

DANA

I like the sound of the inner course. How soon can we start?

DAVID

As soon as you're ready.

DANA

I would like to start now.

DAVID

(On intercom)

"Tami, hold all my calls until I cum – out."

In my mind, I thought this is TV star Dana Plato, and we are going to have sex after knowing each other only 30 minutes. Successful people know what they want and how to get it. Dana and I both thought alike.

I wanted things to be as much a turn on for Dana as they would be for me. She slowly walked towards me and I got up to meet her halfway in the middle of the office. First, I nibbled on her ear. Then we softly and romantically kissed each other on the lips. I bit her lip gently in between our kisses heightening our arousal, making us crave and need more, driving me to take her into my arms. So I walked her backwards to my desk, clearing a portion of it as I picked her up and set her down on it, never breaking apart our lips as if we were glued to one another. My left hand was now cupping and squeezing her right breast. My right hand glided up her inner thigh making her moan and squirm with excitement. Her hands made their way down my abdomen to my belt buckle. She unfastened my pants as I groaned with excitement, my pants dropping to the floor.

I pulled up her skirt and yanked her panties down. She grabbed hold of my now excited, hard shaft and started stoking it up and down. I began sucking on her nipple, making her moan out loud. Her ass started to wiggle on my desk! So I decided to roughly spin her around, bending her over my desk, breathing fast and heavy. I started fingerfucking her ass and she started pumping my finger.

I could not control my excited, throbbing cock and I shoved it inside her. *"Oh yes,"* she moaned. Soon my office was filled with the sounds of my thighs slapping against her ass, and her sexy moans crying out for more. I began spanking her ass hard as I realized she had cummed. I laughed and began spanking her ass harder, and she happily accepted it all. She begged me for more, faster and harder until I couldn't hold back any longer. I had to explode with my legs shaking. I cummed inside her with one last moan from her, "GOD. YES."

This was more than just sex. We were two professionals closing a business deal. Afterwards, Dana and I talked for a long time. We covered every relevant topic, and we also talked about the future. We put together a plan to get her back into her acting and also help her with a singing career. Then I had my limo driver take Dana home.

The next day at the office Dana and I were ready for the world. She came into the office with a smile. She said with me she experienced the sequel to Noah's flood. Sometimes Dana would join in when I was having sex with someone else. Dana was very bisexual. Sometimes she even loved women more. She told me sometimes she felt like a lesbian. I told her that that's another thing that we have in common. I told her that I'm a lesbian caught in a man's body. I hate men and I only do women. She thought that was funny. She also told me that she had a bull dike lover (a heavy female that dresses really butch). Dana was very submissive within oral sensation. She loved sucking men and women, women even more.

All the people in my circle, or kingdom as some would say very much enjoyed this lifestyle. If a man enjoyed variety, why shouldn't a woman have the same right without being labeled?

Dana and I had a discussion on the subject of double standards and labels.

She asked me, *"Why do men have all the fun and are labeled playboys, but a woman doing the same thing gets labeled a whore?"*

I explained, *"A long time ago, prostitution was legal. When men would see their sisters, girlfriends, and female friends being able to have all the sex they wanted, they became very jealous and decided to make it illegal and to make females feel guilty for doing what they couldn't. If a woman pays a man for sex, he would think it was the greatest thing in the world. But if women do that, people look down on them. All the laws against sex are about male jealousy."*

Dana agreed so much about what I had to say that she wanted to write a book with me about sexually repressed society and double standards.

There was the time I took a wooden paddle from a racquetball and made a red mark on Dana's butt. I think she liked it. This is one of the best spanking tools because it makes a loud smacking noise and spreads the pain out evenly. Dana said she loved the way it made her tingle inside. She said it made her want to have sex. She said she was bad and asked for another.

I told her, *"If you are bad, I will punish you with the double dildo."* A double dildo penetrates both orifices at the same time. It looks like a horse shoe. Dana looked at it. Then she said she had never seen one of those before. She asked what she was supposed to do with that thing. I thought to myself if only Dana's fans could see her now. She looked like a mega whore in heat just holding it. After the best sex I've ever had, we held each other in bed and she passed out. I just held her in my arms.

DANA

I've been bad. Can I please have another?

DAVID

I originally put Dana to work interviewing my models for me. She was in charge of Dreamgirls modeling magazine. We would either end up with new talent and sometimes one hell of a great threesome. I had Dana do a promotional video for the new girls to watch. This VHS tape of Dana recruiting girls was digitized in 2020. Jessie posted ALL VHS tapes of her and Dana to YouTube.

It was so nice having Dana around the office. She had reached her lowest point when she was arrested. But this gave her the chance to make the talk show rounds. It was a great moment in history about how to help TV kids in hard times. I was so proud to watch her do these interviews, especially Geraldo.

The girl who played Wednesday on the *Addams Family* was also on the Geraldo show. Jeff from *Father Knows Best* set up a Foundation to help child stars who had lost their careers.

Dana's talk show appearances to discuss her arrests gave my company some recognition and credibility. Dana would wink at the camera, but she said it was for me. She didn't want the public to know she was in a relationship. It helps a career if fans think a star is available. Dana would call me her best bud in the whole world. She would say she really, really loved me.

One of the girls who came into my agency had just turned 18 and we had sex many times. She even brought her girlfriend to join us. I set her up with some powerful people in California. Years later, she changed her name to Jenna Jameson and became one of the biggest porn stars in the world. When I met her, she was Jenna Marsoli. I was the first to do nude pictures of her. She wasn't just good. She was great.

A woman named Crystal had a husband who was a cop, and she wanted me to fix her up with someone that had money to get away from her husband. When her husband found out that she was sleeping with me and getting fixed up, he wanted revenge.

One of Crystal's girlfriends called Lisa, who I was also sleeping with and fixing up, got arrested on drug charges. Crystal's husband persuaded Lisa to try to set me up in exchange for having her own charges dropped. So one day Lisa came by my office and started asking me questions such as *"Was there anybody to be fixed up with for money?"*

I said, *"I know people I could fix you up with, but I have nothing to do with any money."*

So she said, *"Do you think I could get $50 if I gave the guy a blow job?"*

I said that would be between you and him. She then said, *"Well, do you think I could at least make $50 bucks?"*

I was in a hurry and had to leave, so I said, *"Probably."*

She was wearing a wire, and I said probably. That gave the Las Vegas police probable cause to arrest me.

When the police raided my place, two of the cops went into Dana's office and said, *"Dana, let us escort you out of here. You are in the wrong place at the wrong time."* The cops were being nice to her because her attorney was now the district attorney.

The Las Vegas police destroyed my back yard during another raid where they found nothing. They destroyed my ten bedroom estate. They put me out of business for a year during the trial and then found me not guilty. That's why I moved to Arizona.

STEVEN (FROM NEW YORK)

Dana didn't commit suicide. She was murdered. I met Dana Plato at a hotel in Vegas. She was smacking a slot machine out of frustration. I recognized her. We had a great conversation. She was a real rebel, just like me. She would steal tips off tables. She was very money hungry. I loved Dana for her bisexuality. She gave me a kiss as she said goodbye. I would have married her if I could.

I talked with her son, Tyler, over the phone about three times. When Dana died, I bought Tyler a PlayStation and T-shirts. I spent about $500 on Tyler. My friend, Tray, has a lot of footage of Dana. When they were in a relationship, Dana wanted him to take pictures of her doing naked snow angels. But Tray refused; he felt that it was beneath her to take nude pictures.

I liked Erin Moran from Happy Days, but I wasn't in love with Erin. But Dana, I would have had babies with Dana. I hope no one bashes her. She was so misunderstood.

After Dana's death, I was in so much pain. I got a call from a psychic saying she got my number from Dana's spirit. Dana's spirit didn't want me to be in pain any more. I told the psychic to prove herself. The psychic was able to tell me the exact picture I had on my screen saver. I loved Dana so much that her spirit actually contacted me through a psychic.

DAVID

Dana's boyfriend in 1999, Robert, videotaped her after she overdosed. He didn't help her. He came to her funeral and tried to videotape her in the coffin, and they kicked him out. But he was never charged with any crimes.

On the Howard Stern Show, Dana said she didn't do drugs. A caller said she was an old hag and a drug addict. There were many negative callers in fact. So that's when Howard set up a drug test for her. At first, she assured everyone she would do Howard's drug test. She agreed to the pee test. But then she suddenly refused to do the hair test. She cried and begged not to do the hair test. It was the very next day that she overdosed. It was right around that time. I believe she killed herself from what took place on the Howard Stern Show.

4. I Taint Be Unloyal

Goldie Hawn in David's backyard on the set of Wildcats

DAVID

My estate had been used back in 1986 for the Goldie Hawn movie Wildcats. At this set, I met actors and I wore a shiny watch that had 750 diamonds and cost $250,000. I also had a Rolls Royce limousine. Because I looked like a big shot, two young actors were bugging me to be friends with them. I ignored them thinking they were little people. Those two actors later turned out to be Woody Harrelson and Wesley Snipes. I had told them to go hang out with the little people. Hey, I had two beautiful girls on me! I had a driver and a limo. Everyone hated me.

During this time, one of my B movies called 'Las Vegas Blood Bath' was voted the most tasteless movie of all time. And I was voted best producer of low budget films.

There are two things about my movies you should know:

1. If you saw it, you'll remember it for the rest of your life. I can do any type of movie, but I enjoy making slasher movies with a bizarre sense of humor.
2. If you got a speaking part in a low budget movie, you could go to bigger things in Hollywood. However, if you were an extra in a major movie, it would do nothing to help you with a speaking part in a regular movie.

When I was doing movies, girls would fly in from LA, pay all their own expenses, not ask for any pay and have great sex with me. After their speaking role, they would say,

"Thank you so much and can you help my friend in your next movie?" That's also the norm for Hollywood.

During the early 90s, we were getting over 200 girls a week who'd come in to join our agency. The modeling agency was called *10+ Modeling*. The name of the agency came from a movie called *Ten* starring Bo Derrick. Ten is considered a perfect girl, so 10+ meant better than perfect.

Every once in a while we would get a girl who called up and said they were a size 20 and asked if they could come into our agency. We would answer, *"You can come in minus 10."* Like yeah, you have to cut yourself in half or have a split personality.

I remember one time I asked a girl if she would like to lose 20 lbs. of ugly fat. She said yes. I said, *"Cut your head off."*

We did have a lot of heavy girls call so I came up with an idea. Everyone knows Hugh Hefner, founder of Playboy magazine. We were going to have a nude magazine for heavy girls called Hugh Heffer.

A lot of modeling agencies are fronts for photography studios. They would say, *"You have a great look but you need pictures, and we can do that for only $1000."* Legitimate agencies like the one I ran did the pictures for free. We made money from getting the girls work.

It's a catch 22. If a girl is a model, she usually cannot get enough work to support herself. And if she works, she wouldn't have the time to model. I came up with the idea to 900 Dream Girls Modeling Publication: girls got their pictures done for free, get their own 900 extension number put in the magazine and get a dollar per minute to talk to their fans. Even if they talked for just 2.5 hours a day, they would make $1000 per week.

Our computer would send the calls to their cell phone. I made $2 per minute on each girl. We had $200 girls in the magazine. In a short time, we were taking in $50,000 per week. Everything was first class. The girls had a limousine to drive them around, and they had their own hair and nails salon called Utopia. My hair and nails were done almost every day. We even had our own 10+ charge card.

There was a girl who worked at my bikini carwash who looked like Tina Louise from Gilligan's Island, only she had a smaller waist and bigger breasts. She said she was getting married in a few days and blew her rent money. She propositioned me for financial help. I was getting on top of her when she said, *"Can you do me a favor? I want to be loyal to my husband. Can you fuck me in the ass instead?"* In her mind anal was loyal. I thought to myself if my wife on my wedding night was only fucked in the ass, it wouldn't be a sign of loyalty. I taint be unloyal.

Many people wonder about the definition of the word 'taint.' A taint is that flap of skin connecting the groin to the butthole.

At this time, I was also running a couple of dating services. One of them was called *Gold Diggers*. This was a very classy service that catered to beautiful models who wanted to be fixed up with the rich and famous. Our clientele included celebrities, judges, attorneys, movie moguls and the very rich. Joining this service was like buying a Rolls Royce: if you had to ask the price, you couldn't afford it. Nobody was looking for marriage. The girls wanted financial support, and the men wanted to make love to a beautiful model. Some guys even paid for boob jobs of these models. Fixing up the super wealthy with gorgeous models turned out to be a very lucrative deal.

Most of these men were looking for a beautiful model to have fun with, and they didn't mind helping the models financially. The girls didn't want a relationship and were very open-minded. The thought of sex with no catches and financial help was a big appeal to the girls. We had the prettiest girls in any dating service. Almost every girl in *Gold Diggers* knew if they partied with me, I would fix them up with the men with the most money.

The service was extremely successful, so much so that the girls would come onto me just to be fixed up with the best. I had over 100 girls sign up in the first 60 days. I did have the chance to sleep with most of them, but there just weren't enough hours in the day to fit them all in. However, there were ten regulars I saw all the time. There was a secret room in my office complex. I had a clothes rack that when you pulled on it, would open up a wall panel and then you could see the door to the room. It was soundproof. The walls had florescent paint with a black light; it was awesome. There was an expensive sound system and a round bed in the middle. No frame and no chair so that anyone that came in could only sit or lay down on the bed. I also had security cameras all over the office so I could monitor what was going on.

Sometimes I would watch people looking for me. There were only about three employees that worked for me who knew that the room existed. During this time Anne was still my girlfriend, and I was separated from my wife Rebecca who was also trying to get back with me. My lifestyle was very hard for Anne to handle. When Dana came into the picture, Anne felt secondary to her.

During this time I also had many regulars or what you can call friends with benefits. There was Janelle, a gorgeous blond – great body and a very good singer. There was Phillis; she was one of my managers, about 5'4" and a little older; she had a killer body and was also try-sexual (would try anything). She got paid extra to find girls to party with us. Phillis also fixed me up with her gorgeous friend. There was the time two of my girls got into a cat fight. Vanna was threatening to tell Phyllis' boyfriend about Phyllis' dating. Vanna's boyfriend happened to be a famous newscaster.

So I decided to tell Vanna that a friend of mine was flying in to meet her. He wanted anal. Vanna said she didn't do anal. I said he is also a black man. She replied that she didn't do black men either. Then I said the pay is $500. Then Vanna answered, *"My ass belongs to him."* I made a recording of Vanna saying, *"My ass belongs to him"* and gave the recording to Phyllis to use as blackmail.

Phyllis threatened to give the recording over to Vanna's newscaster boyfriend. Well, that shut Vanna up quick.

Vanna never threatened to tell anyone's boyfriend anything after that. During this time, it was not uncommon for me to sleep with three new girls a day. I have a saying, *"I can sleep with three girls once, but I can't sleep with the one girl twice."* And that's in the same day, not in a lifetime. A lot can be said about variety. Some might be thinking, where was Anne, my girlfriend? She enjoyed living with me and having all her bills paid. She let me do whatever I wanted. She didn't create drama. There were no secrets. Plus, she could join in anytime she wanted.

One of my favorite regulars was a former Miss America. Besides the new girls, I had about 20 regulars. I only hung around women who did not believe in those double standards about sex, (I mean they didn't feel guilty about sex and didn't think that only men could enjoy it.) were bisexual and free spirited and open minded.

My ex-wife was a first runner up for Ms. America. Ms. stands for a title of respect for women who don't want to say if they are married. Ms. doesn't mean multiple sclerosis. I'm clarifying this because I wouldn't want people to think I date Multiple Sclerosis pageant contestants or something.

There were many other girls I had a good time with. Another one of my favorites was a former beauty pageant queen. Her name was Tiffany from Illinois. Then there was Bianca who was in the adult industry.

Thinking back, it was amazing that I had time to eat or even breathe. There's something about variety, it is the spice of life. My lifestyle was what guys dream about. Everything was in complete harmony. We were making money and everyone was fulfilling their fantasies without being judged. The two biggest causes of breakups are financial problems and sexual boredom. If there are no financial problems and both people can fulfill each other's fantasies without judgment, then there are greater chances that the relationship would last a long time.

Nothing I did was a secret. When people know what you are into, they can either accept it or not get involved. In a way, my lifestyle was like a restaurant. One has a long line to get in, and the other has no waiting line. Most people get in that line assuming it is better. It's the same with two guys. One is single, and the other is surrounded by gorgeous women. Women think that if the single guy can't get a girl, why should it be me? On the other hand, women want to be with the guy that everyone wants.

I had many other beautiful regulars. There was Ivy, 18, with a girl next door look. She had long brown hair and a perfect body with great boobs. She'd just had a baby. The father took off. I helped her financially. In my world, my age did not mean anything. A girl was either legal age or not. If she was under the legal age, she did not exist to me except for legitimate work.

I was around 40 at that time. When I was 50, I had a 21-year-old girlfriend. My ex-wife, Rebecca, told me how that was not the right thing to do, that I was too old to date so young. She said to someone, *"Can I ask you a question? What would you call it when a 50-year-old man has a 21-year-old girlfriend?"* The man looked at me, and his answer was, *"I would call that very lucky!"*

Moral of the story is that people are jealous of you if you can have or do something they can't. Although it seems like all I did was sex – that isn't true! Sex was just one part of my lifestyle where working was not a business but a way of life. I had many businesses. I made two million dollars from a one week display of a jet version of a car that was used in the movie *Octopussy.*

One of my hobbies was martial arts. In fact, I created my own style. It's called the sting of the scorpion. I spent a couple years at a Chicago monastery called the *Green Dragon Society* that was a Shaolin temple. I had black belt training and this teaching was superior to anything that I had learned before. I also formed the *Black Scorpion Society* which included many self-defense arts.

In 1985 I was appointed deputy sheriff by the mayor of Chicago. I got to carry a badge and a gun. For this honor I had to work one Saturday per month as a bailiff.

What got me into self-defense was the time when somebody threatened to kick the shit out of a friend of mine. I said to that guy, *"Why don't you fight me instead?"* I was sticking up for my friend. Before we started fighting, the police came and broke it up. A person that knew the bully said I was lucky that I didn't fight him since they knew the bully was a black belt. He said to me, *"You'd probably have gotten beaten up."* I figured I better learn self-defense because I never want to be in a position where I couldn't defend myself or somebody that I was with.

At the time I met Dana, I had just finished my fourth movie. In most of the movies, I would write and produce as well as direct. I was developing a reputation for being able to do a movie with any budget – big or small. A lot of wannabees might start a movie, but a lot of them would never finish.

One of my friends was a famous songwriter – Mike Gardener. He had told his close friend about me. I received a call from one of Hollywood's biggest legends, Mickey Rooney. The biggest thing Mickey and I had in common was that we were both married 7 times. Mickey had some movie projects that he wanted to do, and he wanted to make sure that if we went forward that they would not run out of money.

After talking to Mickey for a while on the phone, he convinced me to fly to California to meet with him. What an honor! I met him in his office. Mickey told me the highlights of his life. He had so much energy! He was jumping from one tabletop to another. He was very animated. Mickey also told me when he was around 8 years old he was working on a set of one of the movie companies. It was 2pm, and he was hungry, so he went to the cafeteria. It was after lunch, and it was dark. In the distance, there was a dim light, and a man was sitting at a table. Mickey walked over to him and observed the man was drawing figures on his sketch pad. *"Hey mister what are you drawing?"* Mickey asked him.

The man said, *"What is your name?"*

"Mickey Rooney.

The man answered, *"Ummm, you see this mouse I'm drawing? I'm going to name him after you."* The man was Walt Disney! This was a great story I heard from Mickey that day!

Then Mickey opened his refrigerator and offered me a great drink that he'd made himself. It was fresh watermelon juice and it was delicious.

I told him he should call it 'Mickey Melon.' He did exactly that. I saw Mickey Melon juice on the market soon after that.

Mickey and I got to talking about a movie project we could do together. Mickey wanted to do a movie about female oil wrestlers. It was a coincidence because I used to own a club called *"B.L.O.W"* for Beautiful Ladies Oil Wrestling. I spent four great hours talking with Mickey and we became great friends. We kept in touch by phone from time to time. I decided not to do any projects with Mickey because listening to what Mickey wanted to do was like hearing an idea for a 10 million dollar movie with a 1 million dollar budget. I never start anything I can't finish. Still, it was such an honor to me that he called me and asked to be my partner.

Here's an example of how I like to save money: I had a friend trying to do a movie scene of a woman committing suicide by jumping from a tall, famous building. That would take a huge budget to do. Instead of going to this famous building and showing the entire stunt, I told them just to show the actress looking up.

Then show a picture of the building. Show her jumping off of a step. Then show her splatted on the ground with some fake blood mixed with our leftover Chinese food sprinkled over her. You see? Much cheaper but just as effective. I did a movie called *American Revenge.* The star was Jimmy Van Patton of the Van Patton family, a very respected family in Hollywood. Jimmy starred in a very popular TV series called *8 Is Enough.* I put over 150 women in a movie with him. My partner with this movie was Charles Epeira from Odex Films. Charles is one of the biggest movie producers in Scandinavia. I contacted him as well as my close friend, George.

George is the only person with both a super bowl ring and an Emmy. I contacted them to help me get Dana's career back on track. I also contacted my close friend Ralph Sentener. Ralph had huge connections which included Michael Jackson and Willy Nelson just to name a few. I was working with Ralph and Michael Jackson's former leasing agent Miles Hertzog.

We were going to release an unauthorized home video of Michael Jackson. For those of you who want to know if Michael Jackson was a child molester or a pedophile, according to these inside sources and my opinion, the answer is yes. You can believe what you want, though. Two things are for sure: 1. He was a talented super star 2. Don't let your kids shower or sleep with Michael Jackson and if he offers you Jesus juice (wine), just say no. I got into a fight with Michael Jackson's ex-girlfriend. She claimed Michael had nothing to do with children. But I'm not sure what planet she was living on to say that. She even called up my girlfriend to try to get me in trouble.

For the release of the unauthorized video of Michael, I ran ads in the National Inquirer that cost 8,000 per ad. That was just for a sixth of a page. My contacts and connections in the movie and music industry were the best in Las Vegas. I made the cover of magazines and many newspaper and TV stories. When my name was mentioned, I was referred to as movie producer David Schwartz.

Every pretty girl that came into my agency wanted my help to get into the movie industry. As soon as you gave most women a script to read or put a camera in their face, they froze up. (If you put a camera or a dick in their face, they would choke.) The number of girls who thought that they could sing is also amazing – some were good at karaoke but acapella was a disaster. Now, the girls who wanted to be in the porno industry – they could sure fuck. So of the three, those were the only ones who knew their talent. As a matter of fact, the only difference between a Hollywood actress and a porno star is that the porn star has sex IN the movie and the actress has to have sex to BE in the movie. There is a reason for the saying *"It's not who you know but who you blow."*

Most casting directors will tell you, *"I have two girls, both for the same part. Both are beautiful, and both are equally talented.*

One is open-minded, the other is not." Guess who he will pick? Even some men in the industry have the same problem. That is why there are a lot of closeted gays in Hollywood.

During this time, I bumped into my third wife, Barbara Rogers, a high-class call girl for the mob. She also dated some members of President Nixon's cabinet. We had not seen each other in five years, and the last time I saw her, she held a gun to my head and said, *"Fuck me, or I'll blow your brains out."* It was a no-brainer. I was happy to oblige.

When I saw her five years later, she was still gorgeous only now she looked like a grown-up Barbie doll. On our wedding night many years ago, I had asked her how many men she slept with before me. Her answer changed my life and my morals. She told me she had been a call girl to the mob and a mistress to the rich and famous. She told me she quit counting after 2,500. She said, *"If that bothers you, we don't have to have sex at all."* It was then that I decided, a person's past is irrelevant. What matters is the present – the life from today on. See what a good guy I am? Her favorite thing for sex was to have mint chocolate chip Haagen-Dazs Ice Cream while smoking pot and getting oral. The combination of all three gave her a very intense orgasm.

She would never keep ice cream in the house because she was always on a diet. So during sex, she would stop and make me go buy it. I should have just brought her to Dairy Queen and had sex in the bathroom. Barbara's love for Haagen-Dazs ice cream was something she shared with my second wife who actually did Haagen-Dazs commercials.

Her line in the commercial was, *"Mmmm Haagen-Dazs. If you can say it, you will love it!"* This was shot in the '80s when Haagen-Dazs was unknown.

The first time we met, Susan was wearing a mink bomber jacket. I told her, *"I really like your jacket."*

She said, *"Thank you."*

I then said, *"I have one just like it."*

She said, *"If that's true then I will burn mine."*

I asked, *"Why?"*

She said, *"If you have one like it that makes this jacket common and there is nothing common about me."*

During the times I ran my modeling agency, I had a pizza delivered by a stunning blonde named Lisa. She asked if she was pretty enough to model. I told her she was the prettiest pizza I ever saw. During this time in my life, I was producing B movies, TV, videos, ran a modeling agency, a publishing company, and the dating service called Gold Diggers. We grossed about $50,000 per week. I had 10 businesses all in the same building complex. It was a super plush building that was formerly occupied by senators.

If I slept with a girl to give her a job, she got the job. I never lied or made false promises. This may sound sleazy. Even in Hollywood a guy sometimes has to sleep with a guy to get a job. I believe in the *"me too"* movement, in that it is wrong to force a woman to have sex. I'm also against pimping. But I think people have made a big thing to be politically correct. There is too much political correctness today. In some ways I'm the opposite of the *"me too"* movement because I believe that a woman should be able to use her body to get what she wants – it is all good as long as it's consensual. I wouldn't do away with all casting couch types of relationships entirely. This may be an unpopular opinion, but I also think some parts of the *"me too"* movement are only for ugly women who want to try to get rid of the advantage that a prettier, more sexually open-minded girl may have.

5. I Hear You're the Man

DAVID

Some people think I was successful because I thought outside of the box; I was successful because I thought what would it take to be inside of the box.

I have experienced everything life has to offer – from wealth to prison, and from health to being stabbed in the heart with a ten-inch butcher knife. People have called me the most interesting person in the world and for sure one of the luckiest. I've been with some of the most beautiful women in the world – from beauty queens to TV stars, from porno queens to playboy bunnies to penthouse pets. I've owned Roles Royces, movie theaters, clubs, and am a movie and music producer. I even manufactured my own automobile and distributed my own cola nationwide. I am not a writer, but I do have a story to tell. I do have a purpose in life. I believe you can't have success without failure. The more you fail, the closer you are to success. I believe religion is about control and money. Strong people will do the right thing without being threatened with going to hell. Jealousy is insecurity.

It takes a big person to say they are sorry and an even bigger person to accept an apology. If you catch your woman having an affair and you break up with her, you just gave someone else a great gift. Never look back in the past or too far in the future, but live only in the present. If you don't turn your enemies into friends, they will come back to hurt you one day. Get even by being successful.

JESSIE

I promise one day I'm going to take David to an SA meeting. And I think the *"me too"* movement is the greatest thing that's ever happened to the planet.

DAVID

After all these girls, there was Jessie – the girl who lived with me and Dana in the swinger's club. She will always be my little princess. We were both chasing people we couldn't have. I was chasing her and she was chasing gay guys in the theatre. My greatest accomplishment in life was having sex with this Virgin Mary.

JESSIE

When I first met David, I thought he was a cute Ron Jeremy looking type. I was among the many who answered his ad.

The day of the interview David instantly put me to work answering the phone at his front desk. He could tell that I was not very open-minded. David was good to me. I remember how he made me laugh with his monster mask peeking around the corner.

When I got home from the phone shift, there was a message on my machine. It was David saying he thought he was falling in love with me. Then he added that he thought this wasn't a good thing.

DAVID

I drove to see Jessie's play at the theatre. I was annoyed that she had a kissing scene with some clown. The cops pulled me over for swerving. They even had me walk a straight line and do all kinds of things. I thought I was busted for DUI for sure. But the cop took a call and let me go saying it was my lucky day.

JESSIE

At this time I was acting a small part in a theatre made up of mostly gay guys. It was obvious I guess, but I was slow to wake up to the fact. I also had a boyfriend named Phil, but David convinced me that I should break up with Phil. David said that Phil could do nothing to promote a career for me like he and Dana could. Then David invited me to move in to the club's living quarters and be the boss' girl exclusively.

Right away, I found the committed relationship with David

difficult as he was too much of a taskmaster. And every time we had sex, he would joke, *"Quick. Give me your face."*

That just wasn't my idea of romance. I need a man to hold my hand a while. I need a goodnight kiss. Even Quagmire from Family Guy knows how to do standard operating procedure. Not David.

David skips first base, skips second base, and skips third base too.

So one night I snuck out of David's place and spent the night with a gay actor from the theatre, Kevin. I thought Kevin and I were in love, but he broke it off after only one night saying I wasn't his type or something. I did think it was odd the way Kevin stuck his butt out at me that one time as if he wanted me to wear the dick or something.

Anyway, David found out about it and threatened to throw me out if I didn't break off ties with that theatre.

DAVID

Jessie and I certainly were an odd couple. We're like the exact opposite of each other.

JESSIE

I did a lot for David and Dana. Let me count. I broke up with Phil, I abandoned the theatre, I stayed at the club even after David demolished my car, and I worked the front desk like a slave. I went all in for David and Dana. I sacrificed tirelessly for them both.

When David found me on Facebook in 2017, I was so happy I never killed him! I threw my arms around him and said, *"We should both be dead, yet we live!"* I had never been so happy to see anyone alive before.

DAVID

Well, Jessie didn't attempt to kill me, but I did get stabbed in the heart by a girl named Tish. She used a ten-inch butcher knife. But I survived the trip to the ER. It was nothing short of a miracle. Whenever anyone asks me if I'm a vet, I say, *"Yes, I'm a veteran of seven marriages. I've been stabbed twice and hit with a baseball bat. I've had more injuries than your average military veteran."* Today I meet with Jessie to collaborate on this book. I have to have sex with someone right before my appointments with her just so I will be able to behave myself around her.

JESSIE

David apologized for the times I felt mistreated by him and I forgave him. He showed me this picture of me doing the Jessie James character for his venue back at his 1994 club. It looks like it was autographed by me saying, *"I love you, David, for teaching me right."* I find that very disturbing. What did David teach me that was right?

**1994: These three pictures of Jessica True were shot by David's
personal photographer**

David is my best friend forever. I think of David every time
I hear his favorite song *"In the Air Tonight"* by Phil Collins.

Around 1997, we spent the weekend at David's parents' estate in Las Vegas. His mother pressured him in a heavy,

Jewish accent, *"What makes your swinger's club better than the other ones?"* So, you can understand how David turned out the way he did.

DAVID

My parents were open-minded and never judged me. I was very ambitious and shrewd. That's a killer combination. So, I was the one who took over my Dad's salon business and made us all millions. If I can think it, I can do it. There is no one like me.

It was around 2000 that I started the all-girl band called Goddess X.

I wanted to include as many pictures of Dana as I had taken of her including the one I took of her breasts before her plastic surgery. A star actually posing nude is never as good as catching a star off guard in the nude.

I will always remember the morning I got a call from a close friend of mine back in the early '90s. This was the phone call that started it all. He was good friends with the entertainment director of the Rio. He said, *"Can you do me a favor?"*

I said, *"Sure, anything for you."*

Turns out, he wanted me to give somebody a job – this somebody was at the lowest point in her life. He said no one will touch her and she's on probation. I told him if it's his friend, I would help. I'll never forget when he told me it was Dana Plato. She had just lost her show at the Rio.

That was the day that Dana Plato and I met for the first time.

Dana's first words to me were unforgettable. She said, *"I hear you're the man."*

Appendix

David Schwartz has just received the professional of the year award for the movie industry based on life time achievements. His accomplishments are now listed in Strathmore's Who's Who Worldwide listing.

STRATHMORE'S WHO'S WHO WORLDWIDE

Professional of the Year -

Entertainment/Movie Production

David M. Schwartz

Title: Entrepreneur, Marketer and President, Semi-Retired

Industry: Entertainment

Type of Organization: Production Company

Major Product/Service: Producing movies and related services

Expertise: With over 30 years' experience, Mr. Schwartz specializes in producing adventure movies. He was integral in manufacturing the Lifestar Vehicle Jet version used in the James Bond movie *"Octopussy."*

Geographic Area of Distribution: International

Affiliations: Past President, Cerebral Palsy Foundation of Nevada; President, Wounded Women Warriors

University/Degree: Some College

Born: August 13, 1953

Hobbies/Sports: Martial arts

Spouse: Nancy

Children: Austin, Brandon, Sterling, Shari, Alexandra

Work History: Previously, Mr. Schwartz served as the president of Soul Cola. He owned DMS Rolls Royce Limousine Service and served as a record producer and president of Mandalay Record Company. Mr. Schwartz produced the movie *"Las Vegas Blood Bath,"*

which was the main movie made in Las Vegas, 1989. He was a partner in The Firm Law Office and served as the president of Festivals USA. He also owned a chain of movie theaters in Nevada and Texas. Mr. Schwartz served as a Kung Fu Master and owner of the Black Scorpion Society.

Honors & Awards: Athlete of the Year, B'nai Brith; USA Jewish Olympic Team

Published Works: Publisher, various entertainment magazines

Dana Plato

Dana Plato was an American actress born in 1964. From 1978 to 1986, she played the role of Kimberly Drummond on the popular television sitcom *Diff'rent Strokes*, and this role catapulted her to fame. However, things took a turn for the worse after Dana left *Diff'rent Strokes* – she found herself struggling to secure acting gigs. She worked in a few independent films and in occasional made-for-TV movies. She also did some voiceover work. She married and had a son in 1984 and divorced in 1990. She lost the custody of her son to her former husband, perhaps due to her substance abuse. Things only went downhill for Dana as she struggled with poverty and criminal charges. Her troubled life came to an early end in May 1999 when she died from an overdose of prescription drugs. She was 34 years old at the time. Her only son Tyler later died in 2010 from a gunshot wound to the head around Mother's Day.

The Screwing of David Schwartz

This is David's comment to his 3-year prison sentence. Cops claimed the swinger's club was a house of prostitution, but the evidence shows that there was an undercover cop pretending to be a hooker who could never get fixed up. Here are some transcripts of the trial.

STATE v. SCHWARTZ

Defendant timely appealed from his convictions and sentences, raising three issues. First, defendant contends that the trial court abused its discretion in denying his motion for directed verdicts of acquittal. To support this, defendant argues that the state did not prove essential elements and did not present substantial evidence for convictions. Second, defendant argues that the state's amendment to the original indictment was prejudicial.

Finally, defendant challenges the constitutionality of the statutes under which he was convicted.

David M. Schwartz (defendant) appeals from his convictions and sentences on one count of illegally conducting an enterprise, one count of keeping a house of prostitution, and two counts of enticement of a person for the purposes of prostitution. We affirm.

FACTUAL AND PROCEDURAL BACKGROUND

In early 1994, defendant rented a house and a building behind the house at 1040 East Indian School Road in Phoenix. Defendant was the sole proprietor of several companies operating from that address, including *"D and D Swingers," "D and D Publishing," "Dream Girls Modeling and Casting,"* and *"The Unknown."*

Defendant generated revenue at the location from two distinct activities, both of which he advertised in newspapers. During the day, the business arranged photograph and videotape *"sessions"* with customers and defendant's employees. These *"sessions"* required defendant's employees to engage in a range of activities with a varying price for the customer. Depending on the customer, such activities included modeling in the nude, acts of masturbation, sexual acts with other employees, and engaging in sexual acts, including sexual intercourse, with the customer. Defendant set the price range at $100 to $300 per hour, depending on the type of activity the patron desired.1

Defendant's *"swingers'"* parties were the second source of income from his business. Defendant charged men $35, couples $25, and women were admitted free of charge if they wore lingerie. At these parties, customers watched defendant's pornographic videos, obtained drinks from defendant's bartender, and could engage in sexual acts with other customers or defendant's employees. Testimony revealed that defendant would pay women to attend the parties, would *"set up"* customers with his employees, and would personally collect the fee from the customer for the sexual acts performed by defendant's employees.

Defendant had several employees that served roles vital to the businesses' operation. Receptionists arranged the photo/video shoots, worked the door at the *"swingers'"* parties, and collected the requisite fees. The bartender served drinks to patrons and the security guards patrolled the parking lot to insure safety. Debbie Lauhoff, defendant's girlfriend, assisted defendant in managing the affairs of the house and supervised the cash intake. Other employees were asked to partake in the photo/video *"sessions"* and have sex with the customers.2

In April 1994, the Phoenix Police Department received an anonymous tip about defendant's activities, whereupon the department engaged in a five-month investigation. Undercover Detective Steffani McMichael was the primary investigator on the case and met defendant for the first time on April 20, 1994. Defendant explained the *"swingers'"* parties to her and offered to pay her $100 a night to attend.